OTHER BOOKS BY SUE JOHNSON

THE GREENWOOD PRESS BOOKLE

The Writer's Toolkit: banish the curse of writer's block
The Writer's Toolkit 2: how to create magical stories
The Writer's Toolkit 3: how to create sparkling novels
The Writer's Toolkit 4: the rainbow body

POETRY

Tales of Trees – with Bob Woodroofe (The Greenwood Press)
Journey – with Bob Woodroofe (The Greenwood Press)
Tasting Words, Hearing Colours (Indigo Dreams)

NOVELS

Fable's Fortune (Indigo Dreams)
The Yellow Silk Dress (Indigo Dreams)

SHORT STORIES

Time to Put Your Feet Up

TEEN FICTION

A Solstice Tale

NON-FICTION

Creative Alchemy: 12 steps from inspiration to finished novel
Surfing the Rainbow: visualization and chakra balancing for writers
Writing Success: poetry, flash fiction & short story exercises

See Sue's website for details of her writing courses, talks and critique service: www.writers-toolkit.co.uk

More information about The Greenwood Press publications can be found at: www.greenwoodpress.co.uk

CURIOUS WOMEN

Sue Johnson

THE GREENWOOD PRESS

First edition: CURIOUS WOMEN

First published in Great Britain in 2017 by:

The Greenwood Press
38 Birch Avenue
Evesham
Worcs
WR11 1YJ

www.greenwoodpress.co.uk

ISBN: 978 0 9957290 0 1

Cover design by Fiverr.com

A CIP catalogue record for this book is available from the British Library.

DEDICATION

This book is for friends and family who are gone but not forgotten.

It is also for those interesting female characters I've glimpsed but never met but who have inspired so many poems and stories.

It is especially for my two grandmothers and the only great-grandmother I remember:

Edith Annie Healy   15.10.1898 – 26.3.1992

Alice Maud Bloss   12.9.1884 – 20.1.1978

Emma Dennett   2.11.1875 – 12.1.1958

CURIOUS WOMEN

CONTENTS

CURIOUS WOMEN

Sue Johnson

THE GREENWOOD PRESS

The Fortune Teller

The chair she offers me is threadbare
 and sticky to the touch.

I watch as she makes a fire
dirty hands place sticks, paper, coal.

She strikes a match. The newspaper catches
burns, twists, turns black.

Wood snaps and crackles as she begins her tale,
throws on a handful of salt.

The flames spark orange. I see ravines and canyons.
A rocky pathway leads to a castle.

The picture changes. She throws on copper sulphate.
Green flames spark. A face rises towards me.

"You see what is to come? You understand?"
 Her dark eyes gleam with malice.

A skein of geese passes the window honking loudly.
I watch as they fade into the gathering darkness.

I turn to reply, find myself alone in a derelict house
beside a fireplace full of cold ashes.

Magic Realism

To escape you
I go into the garden and plant seeds.

I ignore your taunts and plant morning glories,
scarlet runners, orange marigolds.
The feel of crumbly chocolate earth,
the smell of damp grass
the glitter of diamond droplets on fresh mint
comforts me.

I watch the rainbows dance.

Later, I leave the garden bathed in moonlight
and go up the stairs to your bed.
You've been drinking and toss and turn,
muttering in your sleep.

I look out of the window.
The moon shines like a spotlight.
I hurry down the stairs
amazed that plants could grow so quickly.

I hear your voice raised in anger
as I climb the beanstalk
surrounded by stars.

Gangan

"My Pretty Queen," she called me
as she sat in her rocking chair by the kitchen fire
She had a wispy bun of silvery hair,
glasses with round frames
and only wore her teeth 'for best.'
She recited 'Robert the Bruce' word perfect.

"My Pretty Queen" she said
 as Mum changed me into the pinafore dresses
I would wear for school –
one tartan the other dark green
She sang a song about Antonio
and his ice-cream cart.

The following night she sat on my bed
in the gas-lit attic
and told me a story about angels.
My brother, asleep in the other bed, did not wake.
I did not hear her footsteps on the creaky stairs
she had not climbed for several years.

The next morning her chair was empty.
My telling of her angel story
met with tears and disbelief
from Gran, Mum and Auntie.
Gangan had died just after midnight.

Alice

Trapped inside an ice prison
only fragile minutes to escape
before her jailer returns.

Icing sugar snow swirls past the window
carries echoes of faces from long ago
a hint that the magic is beginning again.

A blanket of white stretches
broken only by frosted trees
and skeletal hedgerows.

A house in the distance
could represent safety
but would they believe her rambling tale?

She feels a prickle of unease
between her shoulder blades
hears strange music in her head.

Something flutters down the chimney.
A sooty package
lands in the unlit grate.

She discovers a cake
wrapped in silver paper
with a label that says 'eat me.'

She hears the grating of a key in the lock
bites into frangipani and raspberry.
Her head explodes with sound and taste.

She shrinks.

Story Quilts

"You piece together poems
like I make patchwork quilts," she says
as we drink coffee amid a tangle of satin and lace.
"No planning initially – just random thoughts on a page
like I spread fabric over the table
and choose the best bits for my textile story."

I can see how the fragments of a 1950s
blue cotton summer dress
made for my fourth birthday
and the scraps of an ivory satin wedding dress from 1914
that Auntie Nell never wore
are already forming a story so tightly woven
I'll never escape.

Surreal

I rode the escalator through candyfloss clouds,
fell into the plane next to a black cat in red boots.
I'd missed the in-flight meal.

The cat glared at me with luminous green eyes
and gave me a glacier mint.

                    The film was about goblins.

We landed in India – Delhi I think –
and it was market day.
I smelled patchouli and spices,
felt warm sand under my bare feet.

The jagged toothache snarl of a bell
snatched away my indigo scarf
and flung me towards a wall of ice.

Beatrice

On the day they carried her from the cottage
the sky was cobalt blue
over greening rows of potatoes and beans.
Raspberry pink flowering currant
and sherbet lemon forsythia
glowed in the sunlight like a celebration.

Time span backwards
as I watched the slow beat of a tortoiseshell's wings.
At the edge of my vision I saw her
in a white dress and daisy garland,
no longer frail and confused,
run along the path towards the pig sty.
A giggle that could have been
the bubbling call of a curlew
drifted back to me.

A train passing over the bridge
reminds me we are now on the edge
of upheaval and change.
A century of one family's history
obliterated by greed and progress.
Good growing land buried under new houses
to be haunted by her restless spirit.

Dialect

He sat in the chimney corner
grater-faced and miserable as usual
taking up space
turning the milk sour
upsetting the hens

until he tasted my revenge –
a concoction of berries
collected from the hedgerows
fermented overnight
when the moon was full.

I left him downstairs gasping for breath
woke in midnight chill
to the ghostly creak of footsteps on the stairs
and the scent of lilacs –
his mother's favourite flower.

I wedged a chair under the door handle
lit a candle to banish the darkness
woke later feeling refreshed
with sunlight making barred patterns
on the wooden floor.

He was still there in the chimney corner
still grater-faced in death.
I dragged his body to the lake
weighted his pockets with rocks
and pushed him in.

I danced home with sunshine in my heart
cleared all trace of him from the house
chopped down the lilac tree.

Seventh Birthday

Dad calls her 'Mama.'
I call her 'Grandmama.'
She wears black from veiled hat to lace up shoes
smells of mothballs and extra strong mints.

'Children should be seen and not heard,' she says
but I don't feel like talking today.
My throat hurts from the operation
and my head aches.

She talks about me as if I'm not there.
'She looks so frail, I doubt she'll live to twenty one.'
The word 'frail' tastes of white meringues.
Her voice drips like acid and I can't shut it out.

Mum doesn't say anything but her face is pale
with lips pressed into a straight line.
Her hands scrub the lilac patterned bone china
with savage strokes.

Grandmama takes chocolate ginger from her handbag
and puts it into my mouth without asking if I like it or not.
The chocolate is dark and bitter
the ginger stings my throat.

She takes a fairytale book from her shopping basket
musty as a hymn book with mildew spots on the cover.
There's a picture of a witch in a black pointy hat
and a girl with blonde hair who looks like me.

'She has to dance in red hot shoes until she dies.'
Grandmama's eyes flash green fire
and I wonder if she really is a witch.
Is this how I will die when I'm twenty one?

Later my temperature soars and I toss and turn
see myself in nightdress and red shoes
dancing in a moonlit graveyard.
My throat burns with the taste of ginger.

9

Vintage

I am never far from my dream world
a slow blink, a chance meeting like today
and I am in a place beyond here.

drinking Earl Grey tea from rose patterned china
eating bite sized scones from a plate with a lace doily
as I wait for the magic to begin.

The story weaver sits in black silk dress
and crocheted mittens
ready to tell the next part of the tale.

I feel the pull of an unknown planet
as the brass cogs turn, steam rises
and my kaleidoscope life spins on its axis.

Summer Rain

Summer rain drummed a lullaby
on the shed's corrugated iron roof.
The scent of lavender drifted through the open window.
In my dreams I was a child again, back at Lime Cottage.

I've told endless doctors how it began –
on a night of summer rain when I lost my rag doll Milly.
The last time I saw her she was propped by the hydrangea bush.

I didn't realise she was missing until bedtime.
Gran said we'd look for her tomorrow
when the rain stopped
but all I could think was
'she'll never forgive me for letting her green dress get wet'.

I woke at midnight with a feeling that something was wrong.
The rain had stopped. The full moon shone like a stage spotlight.
I opened the window to look for Milly but she was gone.

A large shape detached itself from the shadows,
squelched in black felt shoes between the lavender bushes.
Milly's malevolent painted eyes glared up at me.

The dog died first. I knew Milly never liked the way it sniffed at her.
The vet said he was poisoned but I know he died of fright.
Nobody took any notice of me. They never did.

Gran died of a heart attack on a stormy night
when she went looking for the cat.
Nobody noticed the strange footprints except me.

Even here in this place they call a hospital Milly haunts me still.
Nights of summer rain are the worst.
I lock the doors, draw the curtains tight
stay on guard with my Bible and sharp scissors
in case she comes looking for me.

11

Something Borrowed

Croydon High Street the summer I was seventeen
when Crosby Stills Nash and Young records played
in shops and at every party I went to
where girls drank sweet Martini and the boys
struggled to open cans of Party Seven.

On impulse I'd bought a white trouser suit
from a boutique called Bus Stop that had a wrought iron
spiral staircase down to the changing rooms.

Flared trousers covered blue suede platform shoes
that increased my height by four inches
A turquoise silk blouse billowed
from beneath the short sleeves of the jacket

but it was the hat – stolen from Mum's wardrobe –
that made the outfit special.
It was a squashy white leather barrow-boy cap
that made me feel more self-assured
at a time in my life when I lacked confidence.

I can remember how heads turned as I walked down
the crowded Saturday afternoon High Street –
how one head in particular turned
and a pair of brown eyes locked with mine.

I marched on, not expecting him to follow.
"You walk fast for a girl," he said
when he caught up with me by The Forum café,
"but it was the hat I noticed first."

Mum reclaimed the hat – and her Blue Grass perfume –
when I got home.
I never wore it again
but my relationship with Rob lasted until Christmas.

Flight

In my new class imagination took flight
as Mrs Penny talked about painting a tree.
I knew exactly what I wanted to paint –
a stormy sky behind a tree foaming with pink blossom.

I mixed paint the colour of a bruise and got to work
created billowing clouds and an angry sky.
A boy with red hair looked at me in fascinated horror.
"Miss, miss, look what she's doing," he shouted.

My painting was torn up and I watched from the corner
as the children worked under Mrs Penny's stern gaze
to produce identical lollipop trees hovering between
a blue stripe of sky and a green stripe of grass.

Forty years later when teaching at a local college
I noticed how one lecturer placed the easels behind him
and the students did a weird painting by numbers game
using his exact shades of paint and brush strokes.

I watched spellbound through the half open door
as a repeating image appeared on the lines of canvases
one wing following another like a squadron of Canadas
as the sky darkened outside the window.

The Owl's Seat

She imagined herself in the owl's seat
a building so overgrown with ivy and bramble
only the domed roof stood out like a bald head.

She'd been told there was no way in
stay away
it's not safe.

It was typical of grown-ups to deny a child fun.

She teased away a tendril of ivy
looked inside.

There was a wooden bench she could sleep on
once she'd squeezed in.
They'd never find her here.

She edged forward
the stone floor ice cold on her bare knees.
The square slabs shifted.
Tilted.
Exposed a hole.

She fell down into the darkness beyond.

They'd never find her here.

witching hour

to the casual observer
we are just an ordinary family
clean white net curtains
no litter or weeds in the front garden

but do not be deceived

when night falls we are
the prowlers in the park
the whisper of scandal in the dark

we are the bringers of nightmares
the dream stealers

on pale mornings
you may see our shadows
slice the gloom
as we head home before sunrise

Perfume

"Je reviens" – "I will return" –
her last words
before death claimed her.

Her voice echoes inside my head
to the rhythm of the hammer beats
as they nail her coffin lid.

After the funeral
I gaze at a landscape bleached of colour
try to coax the fire in her small grate.

Just as the feeble spark ignites to flame
a gust of wind like a ghostly sigh
surges down the chimney and extinguishes it.

I sit in the gathering darkness
surrounded by the scent of violets
and the memory of her cold grey eyes.

Daisies

A field of daisies open to the sun
greets me as I make my escape.
I see you waiting by the hedge.

I remember childhood days on this field
when we spent hours making daisy chains
and crowns of buttercup and speedwell.

I kick off my sandals and walk across the soft grass.
A cloud shadow crosses the sun.
I shiver as my mobile bleeps.

I hear his voice harsh as barbed wire,
focus on the field of daisies
as I'd gazed at last night's moon praying for courage to leave.

His voice rolls like thunder. I press the red button,
toss the mobile into a patch of stinging nettles
and run towards your welcoming arms.

Lily of the Valley

The scent of Lily of the Valley drifts
across the darkening station platform.
A memory of my mother cuts sharp as a knife.
I see her face framed with dark hair,
hear her soft French voice speak of how she met my father
in a wood where those flowers grew
and ever after she had worn their perfume to remind her.

I remember her handbag
the combined scents of leather, face powder and
Lily of the Valley. His name for her.

The man I loved left before our child was born
a memory framed by blackthorn
the chill of February and snowdrops waxy as death.

The scent teases me again. I notice her –
auburn hair bundled into a snood
decorated with silver butterflies.
She wears layers of turquoise over purple Doc Marten boots.
Not my mother's style but the expression in her dark eyes
spins me backwards through the years.

She carries an umbrella with a duck's head handle
just like she said she would.

The scent is as strong as the ties of blood that bind us forever.
A crescent moon rises in a pink and apricot sky
as we leave the station.

A blackbird sings.

dance of dreams

an old time waltz in Cedar Bend
led to Earl Grey tea and English muffins
a tarantella of cupcakes
sugared almond colours whirling
in double time

you are dressed in pink watered silk
in a lavender and vanilla scented ballroom
waiting for a slow foxtrot
to lead you out onto the terrace
so you can gaze at the stars

share loving glances

before the music changes to a lindy hop
that carries you home

Juanita

she was a woman who tasted of apricots and dark chocolate
with olive skin that smelled of orange blossom

her eyes were dark as walnut liqueur

deep pools that changed according to her mood

black and impenetrable as a scrying mirror
or dancing with light
when the sunshine of her smile
emerged from a thundercloud of temper
and she gave me that special look
rustled her red silk skirts
turned the sign on the door to closed
took my hand
and led me through the silver beaded curtain
to the velvet darkness beyond

The Three Kings

She's still here in every fibre
of the smoke and soot stained walls.
Nell spent her days in the low ceilinged rooms
moving from fireplace to range
to bar festooned with dried hops
to serve the beer that was her passion.

The men sitting at the mismatched tables
could have been there ten minutes
or a hundred years.

Sitting by the unlit range you may feel a chill.
Thick red dust coats the black kettle and flat irons.
Does anyone remember the last meal cooked here
before the fire died to ashes nobody has cleared away?

Someone has pinned a Remembrance Day poppy
on the wall.

There is no chance of forgetting Nell.
She's still here.

steampunk

a dark pathway edged with pink hollyhocks
a cottage window lit by a flickering candle flame

the rustle of a silk gown behind me
but when I turn to look

there's no one there

the cottage door creaks open slowly
there's a smell of woodsmoke and lavender

from inside I hear the metronome beat of a clock

see the shadow of a presence
I have no wish to meet

Amelia

she was travelling backwards
one slow inch at a time
down the ladder from her bedroom window

moving awkwardly in unfamiliar clothes
the ones that smelled of lavender and mothballs
she'd found in a trunk in the attic

one slow step at a time clutching her ticket
she followed the dark pathway
over the fields to the station

her smile lit the darkness when she saw him
waiting for her on the platform
as their train to freedom approached

Lot's Wife

After many years they found her petrified body in the desert.

There was talk of her becoming an attraction
at an American theme park.
Instead they brought her to Worcester Cathedral
where the Medusa dreadlocks of her hair
support the roof of the Chapter House.
Her face and body are worn smooth by sand and wind.

I feel uneasy in her presence.
The July day is dark and gloomy,
the pink and green glass windows
bleached to grey by the rising storm.
Thunder rumbles a bass note to the lightning's rhythm.
An eerie light shines where her face used to be.
Deep cracks have formed across the bone white ceiling.

The words of my grandmother come back to me
"Whatever happens in life - never look back."

Stepping Stones

When she was in her cradle
it was the red plastic rattle that comforted her
and the green velvet teddy with one ear missing.

Then, at the age of four
with stories dancing in her head
it was the pink fairy costume that she loved.

At fifteen there was the purple silk dress
that all her friends wanted
and the orange and lime hippy beads.

At twenty five came the white wedding dress
the black pin-stripe business suit
and a sober approach to life.

Now in outrageous middle age
she reaches again for the colours of childhood
and rides away on a scarlet motorbike.

Words

The Kitkat snap of icicles outside the kitchen window
cornflakes in a cracked blue bowl I toy with as I gaze at
faded poppies on the wallpaper
last night's greasy dishes in the sink.

I look beyond to the glittering silver path
that could lead me away from here
focus on the comfort of hot chocolate
as I contemplate a life sticky as treacle.

I can no longer ignore the needle-sharp voice that says:
"Get out, lock the door. Move away from this tissue of lies."

Woodstock

I saved for weeks to buy the triple album
played it constantly on the record player
built by my friend Sam,
the arm weighted by an old penny
glued in place to stop the needle jumping.

I had long hair parted in the middle
wore too much black mascara and pale lipstick
lived in a black kaftan decorated with pink and gold embroidery
bought thong sandals because Mum told me not to.
"They don't look comfortable," she said.
As always, she was right.
I abandoned them in Brighton,
travelled home barefoot.

I wore cowbells, burned joss sticks in my bedroom
got a lecture from Dad about drugs and boys
warning me to stay away from both,
sat on the lawn, eyes closed, trying to meditate
until my brother put a frog in my lap,
wished with all my heart I was old enough
to go to Woodstock and be a flower child.

Mary Shelley

The summer that never was we stayed up late night after night
huddled round the dying embers of the fire
drinking rough red wine, reading ghost stories
that stirred the shadows in that strange villa by the lake.

The men became restless. Bored.
I don't know who suggested the idea.
That we should each write the scariest story we could think of.
'Write to wake the dead.'

That night I woke in a tangle of sheets with the cold eye of the moon
staring in through the half open shutters.
I lay still staring back at it
tried to piece together the tale that haunted my midnight pillow.

Long days later when the tale was written
there were those who called me evil and depraved.
What I would say in my defence is that I did not choose this story.
It chose me.

Haunted

I knew I didn't like you from the start
symbol of everything we'd lost
you were cold and had no heart
touched my very soul with frost.

Symbol of everything we'd lost
a restless spirit stalked my lonely room
touched my very soul with frost
I felt trapped in misery and gloom.

A restless spirit stalked my lonely room
I feared the drawing in of every night
I felt trapped in misery and gloom
my Bible was forever in my sight.

I feared the drawing in of every night
Mum and Dad dismissed my haunting fear
my Bible was forever in my sight
I was certain something evil had drawn near.

Mum and Dad dismissed my haunting fear
you were cold and had no heart
I was certain something evil had drawn near
I knew I didn't like you from the start.

Dream

The lane narrows as I drive along it
reminds me of a horror film where the room shrinks.

A sign says 'no cars on the bridleway.'

There's a scritter of twigs against silver metal.
Yellow pollen gilds the windscreen.
White clouds race across a patch of blue.
There is no way out.

I wake to the sound of a holly blue's wings
against my window
and know your spirit has flown.

Maria

Heat prickles
shimmers like a dragonfly's wings.
Distant thunder crackles.

She gazes at scarlet poppies
outlined by charcoal sky
as she walks the cracked pathway
throat parched
back aching
feet blistered
towards the bleached white cottage
surrounded by a sea of lavender.

Every step she takes is a reminder
that he is gone
and a new life is growing inside her.

She expects no welcome
from her mother
when she arrives.

She prays for rain.

speedwells

jewelled grass starred with speedwells
brings back memories
of playing with the treasures on your dressing table

the scent of bluebells
your silk dress
the colour of your eyes

Gran's Front Parlour

was a place for Sundays
Christmas
and laying out the dead

it was colder than the rest of the house
a place where games were not played
that smelled of beeswax
and the echo of funeral lilies

I wonder if she ever saw echoes
of faces from the past
in the firelit Christmas baubles

Tiffany Glass

The Tiffany glass lamp is the one thing I miss,
thrown in frustration from our cottage door
on the day I discovered you were cheating on me.

Every day since you left with your bulging suitcases
I have searched the shore for scraps of coloured glass
gathering the fragments like jewels.

The shape and colour of the lamp still lives on
in my memory – a circle of dragonflies in perpetual motion
with amber eyes that are so like yours.

In the cold darkness, I remember the touch of your fingers.

Chakra

Red
for sorrow
the joy of my life has ceased.

Red
for the splitting apart
of all my dreams.

Red
for the eyes that weep
the stars will fall from the heavens
the fields are devastated
the landscape of my life is dust
the sun shall be darkened
and the moon will not give me light.

Writing a poem will not
heal the hurt.
The words I bleed onto the page
will not take away my sorrow.

Venice

Harlequin guides her over the narrow bridge
his grip like a chain of iron on her fragile arm.
Mist closes in blocks moon and starlight
muffles sound and distance.

She hears muted music from a palazzo near the water
the dip and splash of oars
a giggle and the trip of dainty footsteps
here and gone stifled by the swirling whiteness.

Her head reels from the wine she was forced to drink –
drugged, you suspect, as her eyes struggle to focus.
"You will not escape." The voice is sibilant
 his breath warm against her neck.

The ballroom is lit by chandeliers that stir in the draught
the changing light makes her feel as if the floor is tilting.
The nightmare dance begins –
all the figures clothed in black, their masks bone-white.

In the corner a card game begins.
They are drawing lots. For her.
She moves down the dance to the wild fiddle's tune
eyes the door, weighs her chances of escape.

Knows she will not.

Science

My mind freezes as I walk an endless school corridor
towards the science lab.
My mouth is dry. The faces of the three bullies
loom in and out
of nightmare strobe lighting,
tongues flickering like snakes.

I seek shelter.

Safety.

I never liked science or Mr Richards
with his bushy ginger beard
but now as I stare up at him
he is my protector.

I gabble a question about magnets
ask why they repel
notice three faces the other side of the fragile glass door
see them dissolve like meringues
as sunlight streams through unfamiliar red curtains.

Foraging

The landscape is dusty green and gold
under blue late August sky

The hedgerows are crammed with blackberries,
elderberries, hawthorn and sloes.

Heat rises from the dried grass as we walk the pathway
between woodland and plum orchard.

There are glimpses of woodland shadow
and I hear children's voices.

A memory stirs of childhood days picking blackberries
and I wonder if I turned to look
would I see an image of myself from long ago
captured in black and white by the old Box Brownie?

The Play

Tight laced in a corset unable to take a deep breath
I stood in the wings of a theatre I didn't know.

I'd followed the call for 'overture and beginners,'
was dressed in buttercup yellow silk, a horsehair wig
and old-fashioned shoes with silver buckles.

I could hear the babble of conversation beyond
the red velvet curtain.
smell the cocktail of perfumes,
sense the excitement as they waited.

I fidgeted as the musicians tuned up,
the cats-yowl whine of a violin, the deeper reply of a cello.
Black-clad figures positioned props on the dark stage –
chair, table, mirror.

I waved to them but they ignored me. The po faced
stage manager walked past me as if I wasn't there.
I followed him. I wanted to know. Needed to know.

"When will you give me my lines?
Tell me what the play is about?
Tell me what I need to say."
I clutched his sleeve. He looked a little scared.

As the curtains opened and his image faded I heard him say:
"The choice was always yours. Make of it what you will."

On the Beach

My aunt helps me into my pink ruched swimsuit
sends me barefoot across blue and yellow pebbles
towards the sea
tells me not to step in any tar
or get it on my clothes.

What she doesn't tell me is
how the swimsuit fills with water
heavy as lead weights around my neck.
I grip the breakwater, look back at men in deckchairs
with knotted hankies on their heads.

I let go of the breakwater to reach for a shell.
A wave knocks me off my feet.
The weight of the swimsuit
drags me down into green water
thick with seaweed.

I struggle upwards towards the light.
Open my eyes to find there is no beach,
no sandcastle decorated with flags
and I am as old as my grandmother.

The smell of tar from the everlasting roadworks
drifts in through the open window.

A giant spider like the steel and basalt one
I sat beside in the orange tree shade
of a Portuguese museum garden
eyes me curiously
as it hangs from my bedroom ceiling.

Its dumb insolence irritates
like fingers scraped down a blackboard.
I struggle out of bed to fetch the feather duster.

My aunt's voice tells me I'm like the old woman
tossed up in a basket ninety times as high as the moon
on a journey to sweep the cobwebs out of the sky.

I'm relieved when she says
they don't wear ruched swimsuits up there
and near the thirteenth star there's a café
where they serve half-moon cake all day.

The Pumpkin Coach

On the day before the summer solstice
I walk Fort Royal Hill after a night of torrential rain
focus on colour, scent and texture

gather images for my notebook
pale blue iris
deep red roses
surrounded by the scent of elderflower and lavender.

I touch the silky petals of an orange poppy.
One falls onto the damp grass
exposes the black seed head at its heart

I press the petal between the pages of my book.

Later when I look at it
I see it is the shape of Cinderella's pumpkin coach
its vibrant colour faded to silver in places.

A pumpkin left to decay
unwanted and unnoticed
after the fairy-tale happy ending.

meditation

somewhere between the worlds
I hang suspended by my breath.

weightless

connected to something far beyond
this world

I see indigo mountains
surrounded by gold leaf sunshine
move towards them
as the yoga teacher calls me back

back

to my place on the attic floor
on soft cream carpet
a view through the skylight
of a purple meringue cloud and black chimney pots

July Full Moon

Cloud the texture of barbed wire
barricades the full moon's face.

All day relentless heat has poured from a too blue sky
as we hugged the shadows
greedy for every breath of wind.

The corn is ripe
sweat trickles
tension crackles.

Now as darkness comes
the wind stirs the branches of the silver birch.
Cloud stacks gather like an invading army

I am too restless to sleep
go into the garden
sit on the bench surrounded by the scent of buddleia,
honeysuckle and lavender
listen to the tinkle of windchimes and the rustle of leaves
watch moths flit like ghosts.

Light years away, pale stars appear
The yellow moon gleams inside its cage.

Monica

Two days before the shortest day of the year I visited you.
Thick fog made me feel as if I was driving
through a narrow tunnel
unable to see anything beyond my headlights
as restricted as your life has been since you had a stroke.

You are in bed when I arrive and are totally changed
from the person I knew last week.
Your chest infection has not cleared. You will not drink
and refuse all food but chocolate.

The flesh has melted from your bones
and your skin is pale as candlewax.
You recognise me and smile as you have always done.
When I leave I wish you Merry Christmas and Happy New Year.

The angel of the resurrection sits in the shadows
waiting to carry you to the light.

The Button Tin

An old Cow & Gate baby milk tin
pewter grey
crammed with buttons cut from cardigans,
shirts and jackets
before the fabric was recycled into other garments,
bags, toys and rag rugs.

Bickering over our favourite ones
we tipped them out on the cream and pink rug
in the sitting room.
It was the quiet time between lunch and
Listen With Mother.

The smell of lamb stew and treacle sponge
hung in the air as we made lines and circles
or sorted them into colours and shapes
until the magic music began
on the old fashioned wireless
and we sat, listening with Mum
in the rose-patterned armchair.

Jellypicklejam

Push open the door
shut out the world
enter the place where magic happens.

Move carefully – notice the signs.

Do not be tempted to follow the rainbow staircase
down to the cellar.

You may not escape.

'Misbehaving children will be sold to the circus.'

It is said that the courtyard outside vibrates to ghostly music
when midnight comes.

A ringmaster once lived here and his spirit lives on.
You only have to look for the clues.

First there is the tented ceiling
made of red and white silk
with an old fashioned birdcage hanging from the centre
crowded with metal butterflies.

Teacup garlands linked with ribbons and pearls
decorate the walls.

Old fashioned knives and forks
that once belonged to Lola the trapeze artist
are trapped in a glass frame.

Watch and listen and the stories will gradually unfold.
Carry them with you always.

23 High Street, Orpington

These were the joys of that garden:

tall hollyhocks in sugared almond colours
an outside loo with a hole in the wooden seat
that led down to Australia if you fell in

a green water butt
where the jewel-eyed toad lived

a laurel bush like a speckled umbrella
where I played with my dolls

the constant tseep-sawp whine of the sawmill
on the other side of the pond
the sound of the lunch-time hooter
and the drifting smell of freshly cut wood

the place at the bottom of the garden
where we gathered sycamore leaves
for pretend dinner plates

the curved stone edgings of the carefully weeded paths
feathery tops of carrots
red bean flowers
orange burn of marigolds

Gran's voice calling us in for lunch.

A Working Duchess

Bet you've never seen the likes of me before.
Rubies, diamonds, sapphires make my world go round.

A working duchess – that's what I am.
There ain't many jobs where you can dress in satin and lace -

not that I wear much most of the time –

just the diamonds and rubies. And some of my customers
prefer me au naturel as the French would say.

As to how I feel about them –
Well, all cats are grey in the dark aren't they?

I close my eyes and think of the money
and the good old Empire
with each creak and rattle of the bedsprings.

I begin each day with oysters and champagne.
Make the most of life as my old Ma used to say.

THE GREENWOOD PRESS

38 Birch Avenue
Evesham
Worcs
WR11 1YJ

www.greenwoodpress.co.uk

Printed in Great Britain
by Amazon